I WANT IT!

LEARNING TO CONTROL YOUR TEMPER

Katherine Eason

FOX EYE
PUBLISHING

Itsuki had **TEMPER TANTRUMS**. When Itsuki felt upset, she cried and screamed and kicked her legs in the air. When she felt angry, she shouted and kicked or threw things.

Itsuki **DIDN'T SAY** how she was **FEELING**. She didn't think it was important.

Itsuki **DIDN'T WANT** to do her homework. She wanted to play in the garden.

Itsuki **CRIED** and **SCREAMED**. She **KICKED** her legs. Dad said the rule was homework first.

Dad asked Itsuki to turn the television off. It was dinner time. Itsuki **DIDN'T WANT TO.** She felt **ANGRY.**

She threw the remote control across the room. Itsuki had **TIME OUT**.

Itsuki wanted Mum to read a story to her. Mum was talking on the phone. Itsuki **DIDN'T WANT** to wait.
She **SCREAMED** and **CRIED**.
She **KICKED** her legs.

Mum said Itsuki must wait until she had finished.

On Saturday, Dad took Itsuki to the playground. When it was time to go home, Itsuki **DIDN'T WANT TO.** She felt **UPSET.**

Itsuki SCREAMED and CRIED.
But Dad took her home.

Later, Itsuki went shopping with Mum. She put some sweets in the trolley. Mum put the sweets back. Itsuki was **ANGRY**.

She **SHOUTED** and **KICKED** the trolley.
But Mum didn't buy her the sweets.

Itsuki had **TIME OUT**. Mum said it was OK to say she felt angry or upset. But it wasn't okay to scream and shout or kick and throw things.

Mum said that Itsuki could have a sticker if she **CONTROLLED HER TEMPER**. When she had ten stickers, she could get a new book.

That week, Itsuki used words to show when she was upset or angry.
She didn't shout or scream.
She didn't kick or throw things.

Itsuki got a new book. She felt **GOOD**. She had learnt to **CONTROL HER TEMPER**.

Words and Behaviour

Itsuki didn't control her temper in this story and that caused a lot of problems.

TEMPER TANTRUMS

ANGRY

CRIED

KICKED

There are a lot of words to do with controlling your temper in this book. Can you remember all of them?

SCREAMED

TIME OUT

Let's talk about feelings and manners

This series helps children to understand difficult emotions and behaviours and how to manage them. The characters in the series have been created to show emotions and behaviours that are often seen in young children, and which can be difficult to manage.

I Want It!

The story in this book examines the reasons for controlling your temper. It looks at why controlling your temper is important and how using words helps people to show how they feel.

How to use this book

You can read this book with one child or a group of children. The book can be used to begin a discussion around complex behaviour such as controlling your temper.

   The book is also a reading aid, with enlarged and repeated words to help children to develop their reading skills.

How to read the story

Before beginning the story, ensure that the children you are reading to are relaxed and focused.

Take time to look at the enlarged words and the illustrations, and discuss what this book might be about before reading the story.

New words can be tricky for young children to approach. Sounding them out first, slowly and repeatedly, can help children to learn the words and become familiar with them.

How to discuss the story

When you have finished reading the story, use these questions and discussion points to examine the theme of the story with children and explore the emotions and behaviour within it:
- What do you think the story was about?
- Have you been in a situation in which you didn't control your temper? What was that situation?
- Do you think controlling your temper doesn't matter? Why?
- Do you think controlling your temper is important? Why?
- What could go wrong if you don't control your temper?

Titles in the series

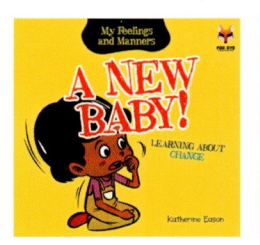

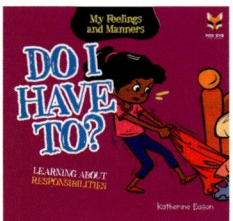

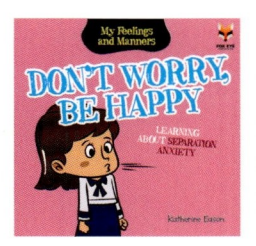

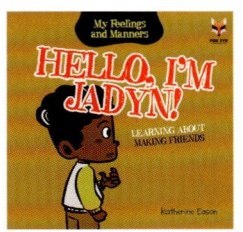

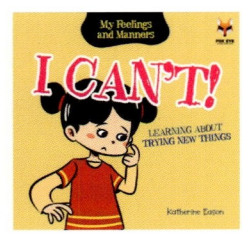

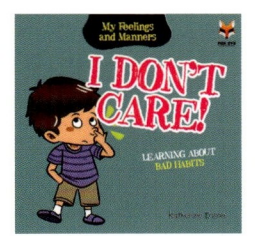

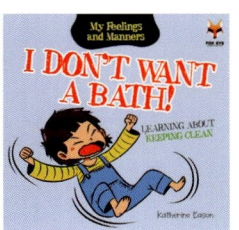

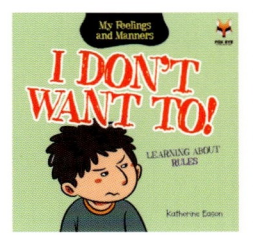

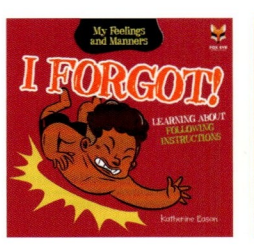

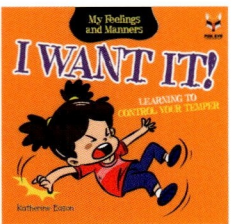

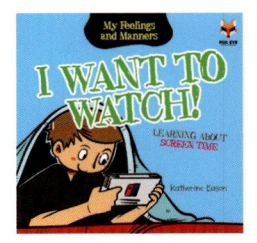

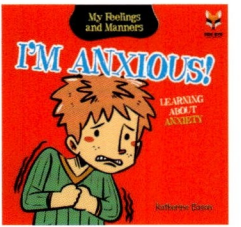

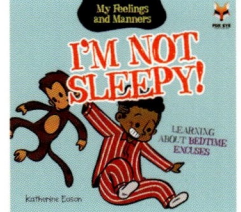

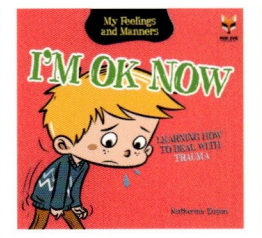

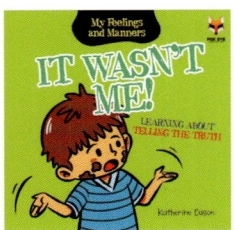

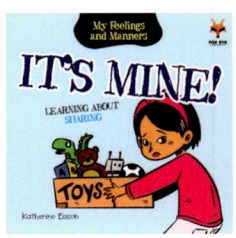

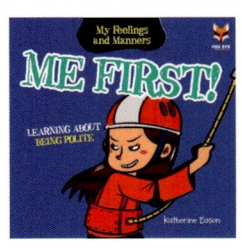

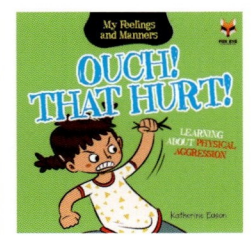

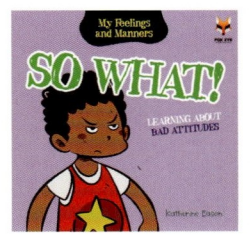

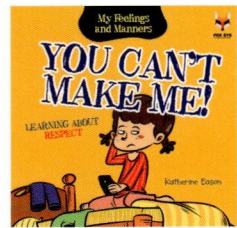

- **A New Baby!** — Learning about Change
- **Do I Have To?** — Learning about Responsibilities
- **Don't Worry, Be Happy** — Learning about Separation Anxiety
- **Hello, I'm Jadyn!** — Learning about Making Friends
- **I Can't!** — Learning about Trying New Things
- **I Don't Care!** — Learning about Bad Habits
- **I Don't Want a Bath!** — Learning about Keeping Clean
- **I Don't Want To!** — Learning about Rules
- **I Forgot!** — Learning about Following Instructions
- **I Want It!** — Learning to Control Your Temper
- **I Want to Watch!** — Learning about Screen Time
- **I'm Anxious!** — Learning about Anxiety
- **I'm Not Sleepy!** — Learning about Bedtime Excuses
- **I'm OK Now** — Learning How to Deal with Trauma
- **It Wasn't Me!** — Learning about Telling the Truth
- **It's Mine!** — Learning about Sharing
- **Me First!** — Learning about Being Polite
- **Ouch! That Hurt!** — Learning about Physical Aggression
- **So What!** — Learning about Bad Attitudes
- **You Can't Make Me!** — Learning about Respect

First published in 2023 by Fox Eye Publishing
Unit 31, Vulcan House Business Centre,
Vulcan Road, Leicester, LE5 3EF
www.foxeyepublishing.com

Copyright © 2023 Fox Eye Publishing
All rights reserved. No portion of this book may be reproduced in any form without permission from the publisher, except as permitted by U.K. copyright law.

Author: Katherine Eason
Art director: Paul Phillips
Cover designer: Emma Bailey
Editor: Jenny Rush

All illustrations by Novel

ISBN 978-1-80445-171-7

Printed in China